JOJO SIWA
Making a Difference on Social Media

By Katie Kawa

KidHaven
PUBLISHING

People Who Make a Difference

Published in 2024 by
KidHaven Publishing, an Imprint of Greenhaven Publishing, LLC
2544 Clinton St.
Buffalo, NY 14224

Designer: Deanna Paternostro
Editor: Katie Kawa

Photo credits: Cover, p. 5 Tinseltown/Shutterstock.com; p. 7 Kathy Hutchins/Shutterstock.com; p. 9 Ga Fullner/Shutterstock.com; pp. 11, 13 Featureflash Photo Agency/Shutterstock.com; p. 15 MediaPunch Inc/Alamy Stock Photo; p. 17 GrandAve/Shutterstock.com; p. 18 Imagespace/Alamy Stock Photo; p. 20 ZUMA Press, Inc./Alamy Stock Photo; p. 21 T.Sumaetho/Shutterstock.com.

Library of Congress Cataloging-in-Publication Data

Names: Kawa, Katie, author.
Title: JoJo Siwa : making a difference on social media / Katie Kawa.
Description: Buffalo, New York : KidHaven Publishing, [2024] | Series:
   People who make a difference | Includes bibliographical references and
   index.
Identifiers: LCCN 2023010457 | ISBN 9781534544239 (library binding) | ISBN
   9781534544222 (paperback) | ISBN 9781534544246 (ebook)
Subjects: LCSH: Siwa, JoJo, 2003- | Sexual minorities–United
   States–Biography–Juvenile literature. | Internet personalities–United
   States–Biography–Juvenile literature. | Dancers–United
   States–Biography–Juvenile literature.
Classification: LCC HQ73.2 .K39 2024 | DDC 306.76092 [B]–dc23/eng/20230322
LC record available at https://lccn.loc.gov/2023010457

Printed in the United States of America

Some of the images in this book illustrate individuals who are models. The depictions do not imply actual situations or events.

CPSIA compliance information: Batch #CSKH24: For further information contact Greenhaven Publishing LLC at 1-844-317-7404.

Please visit our website, www.greenhavenpublishing.com. For a free color catalog of all our high-quality books, call toll free 1-844-317-7404 or fax 1-844-317-7405.

Find us on

CONTENTS

A SOCIAL MEDIA STAR

Young people can make a very big difference in the world around them. One of the ways to do this is through social media—the collection of websites and applications, or apps, that allow people to connect with each other and form online communities. Young people use social media to spread the word about important causes, share their stories, and help each other feel less alone.

One young person who uses social media to make the world a better place is JoJo Siwa. Her posts **inspire** people around the world to dream big, be themselves, and be kind to one another.

In Her Words

"Nothing I've ever done has been something I didn't want to do … If I wanted to create an alternate identity [a different person to be], I could do that—it'd be easy. I didn't. This is me."

— Interview with the *New York Times* from September 2021

As of early 2023, JoJo Siwa had more than 11 million followers on Instagram, more than 45 million followers on TikTok, and more than 2 billion views on her YouTube channel! She uses those **platforms** to share things about her life as a dancer, a singer, a TV star, and a member of the **LGBTQ+ community**.

5

DANCING INTO THE SPOTLIGHT

Joelle Joanie Siwa was born to dance. In fact, her mother, Jessalyn, was a dance teacher! JoJo was born on May 19, 2003, in Omaha, Nebraska. Ten years later, her dancing helped make her a star on a TV show called *Abby's Ultimate Dance Competition*.

JoJo then joined a TV show called *Dance Moms*, which followed a group of young dancers and their parents. She appeared on the show as a dancer from 2015 to 2016. In 2015, JoJo also started her own YouTube channel, where she shared vlogs, or short videos about her life.

In Her Words

"You can dream a dream and make that dream come true, no matter what."

— Instagram Live video from January 2021

On *Dance Moms*, JoJo was known not only for her talents as a dancer, but also for her big **personality** and for the way she often said exactly what she was thinking.

BULLIES AND BOWS

JoJo began speaking out about issues that were important to her at a young age. In 2016, she released, or put out, her first song. "Boomerang" is a song about bullying, especially the kind of online bullying known as cyberbullying. With this song, JoJo inspired her fans—called Siwanators—to believe they're stronger than any bullies they might face.

JoJo has continued to take a stand against bullying. She's spoken openly about her own experiences with bullies and mean people online because she hopes it can help her fans feel less alone.

In Her Words

"When you see a kid or someone wearing a JoJo bow, you know that they're a Siwanator, which means they are kind, they are nice, they are strong, they are powerful, they love everyone, they support everyone, they want to be your friend, they want to be everyone's friend."

— Interview with the *Today* show from May 2019

When she was younger, JoJo was known for wearing big bows in her hair. In 2016, Claire's stores started selling official JoJo Siwa hair bows. JoJo has said that wearing one of her bows means you stand against bullying.

POSITIVE WORDS

JoJo's music has continued to spread positive messages. In 2017, she released the songs "Kid in a Candy Store" and "Hold the Drama," which was another song about not listening to mean people. A year later, she released her first album—*D.R.E.A.M. The Music*. That was followed by another album in 2019 (*Celebrate*) and a Christmas album in 2020.

JoJo inspires her fans with the words of her songs and also with the words she writes in her books. Her first book—

JoJo's Guide to the Sweet Life: #PeaceOutHaterz—came out in 2017. Since then, she's **published** many other books for young people.

In Her Words

"Remember, nice is awesome. It's not about being the most popular kid in school or having the best clothes. It's about being happy with who you are and how you treat other people."

— *JoJo's Guide to the Sweet Life: #PeaceOutHaterz*

JoJo went on tour to sing her songs in front of her fans in 2019.

ON TV

JoJo's concerts weren't the only places her fans could see her. Her face seemed to be everywhere by the late 2010s! She appeared on different shows for the Nickelodeon TV channel, including an **animated** show called *The JoJo & BowBow Show Show* about her life with her dog BowBow.

JoJo also **performed** on *The Masked Singer* in 2020. The next year, she became the first woman on *Dancing with the Stars* in the United States to have another woman as her partner. She wanted to challenge, or push back against, **traditional** ideas about the **roles** of men and women in the world of dance.

In Her Words

"I am so proud to be me."

— Interview with *People* magazine from April 2021

JoJo has been a part of movies too! In 2019, her voice was used in *The Angry Birds Movie 2*. In 2021, she was part of a movie called *The J Team*.

SHARING ON SOCIAL MEDIA

As JoJo's star continued to rise, she continued to connect with her fans on social media. Her YouTube channel—Its JoJo Siwa—has given her fans a closer look at who she is as a person. She's shared videos of herself putting on her makeup, babysitting kids, and getting ready in the morning. JoJo also uses Instagram and TikTok to share videos with her fans.

In 2021, JoJo's YouTube channel began showing videos from her latest TV show—*Siwa's Dance Pop Revolution*. On this show, JoJo and her mom created a new singing group called XOMG POP!

In Her Words

"But with these kids [XOMG POP!], I'm able to help them and guide them and give them advice, but still giving space and allowing them to be themselves and just offering my advice when they need it."

— Interview with *Billboard* magazine from June 2022

JoJo is shown here with the members of XOMG POP! at an event.
JoJo has said she likes being able to make a difference by being a mentor,
or a person who helps and gives advice, to younger girls
like the members of this group.

COMING OUT

JoJo loves to use social media to share parts of her life with her fans. In January 2021, she shared a very important part of her life with them on TikTok and Instagram. She made posts about being part of the LGBTQ+ community, and those posts made headlines around the world.

Telling someone you're a part of the LGBTQ+ community is often known as "coming out." By being brave enough to come out in such a big way, JoJo hoped to inspire other young people to be honest about who they are and who they love.

In Her Words

"It might be harder for some people and easier for some people to come out or be themselves, but I think coming out has this stigma [negative view] around it—that it's this really, really scary thing. But it's not anymore. There are so many accepting and loving people out there that it's OK."

— Instagram Live video from January 2021

JoJo is proud to be a member of the LGBTQ+ community. She hopes living her life openly helps make it easier for younger members of the LGBTQ+ community to feel comfortable being themselves and to feel accepted by the people around them.

17

SPECIAL HONORS

Even before JoJo came out as a member of the LGBTQ+ community, she was seen as someone with the power to inspire young people. In 2020, she was named one of *TIME* magazine's 100 Most Influential People. This list honors people who influence, or have an effect on, others in important ways.

In 2022, JoJo was presented with the Gamechanger Award by GLESN—a group that works to make sure all students, especially LGBTQ+ students, feel accepted and included at school. JoJo was given this honor for the work she does to fight bullying and make the world a kinder place.

In Her Words

"A lot of people get bullied for the same things that I will … I think that is something that I have the power to help people [with]."

— Interview with *Teen Vogue* magazine from September 2022

The Life of
JoJo Siwa

2003
Joelle Joanie Siwa is born on May 19 in Omaha, Nebraska.

2013
JoJo appears on *Abby's Ultimate Dance Competition*.

2015
JoJo becomes a major part of the TV show *Dance Moms* and starts her own YouTube channel.

2016
JoJo continues to be a part of *Dance Moms*, releases her first song ("Boomerang"), and works with Claire's to start selling bows like the ones she wears.

2017
JoJo releases the songs "Kid in a Candy Store" and "Hold the Drama" and comes out with her first book, *JoJo's Guide to the Sweet Life: #PeaceOutHaterz*.

2018
D.R.E.A.M. The Music is released.

2019
JoJo goes on tour, releases the album *Celebrate*, and is part of *The Angry Birds Movie 2*.

2020
JoJo releases a Christmas album, appears on *The Masked Singer*, and is named one of *TIME* magazine's 100 Most Influential People.

2021
JoJo comes out as a member of LGBTQ+ community, creates the group XOMG POP!, and is seen in the movie *The J Team* and on the TV show *Dancing with the Stars*.

2022
JoJo appears on *High School Musical: The Musical: The Series*, and she is honored with GLESN's Gamechanger Award.

JoJo has shown that you're never too young to make your mark on the world!

JUST GETTING STARTED

JoJo is continuing to **represent** the LGBTQ+ community in important ways. For example, in 2022, she appeared on the Disney+ show *High School Musical: The Musical: The Series* as Madison, a member of the LGBTQ+ community.

JoJo is also working to help in the fight against **cancer**. She created the JoJo Siwa Childhood Cancer Foundation to support children with cancer. This is just one of the many ways JoJo uses her fame to help others. She spreads kindness and hope on social media and beyond, and by being proud to be herself, she helps others feel proud to be themselves.

In Her Words

"It's okay to be a little weird, strange, different. That's something we should never, ever be afraid of. That's something we should be proud of."

— Instagram Live video from January 2021

Be Like JoJo Siwa!

If you see someone being bullied or if you're being bullied, tell a trusted adult.

Be true to yourself, and support your friends so they can be true to themselves.

Spread kindness in person and on social media (if you use it).

Tell the truth, even if it makes it harder to fit in.

If someone comes out to you as a member of the LGBTQ+ community, listen to them, and show them they're accepted for who they arc.

Help younger people if they come to you for advice.

If you see someone being picked on for being different, treat them with kindness, and make them feel included.

Raise money for groups that help sick kids.

If you want to be like JoJo Siwa, you can start by remembering that it's cool to be kind!

GLOSSARY

animated: Made using a series of drawings, pictures, or computer-created images that are shown quickly one after another.

cancer: A sometimes deadly sickness in which cells grow in a way they should not, often forming tumors, or growths, that harm the body.

inspire: To move someone to do something great.

LGBTQ+ community: A group made up of people who see themselves as a gender different from the sex they were assigned at birth or who want to be in romantic relationships that aren't only male-female. LGBTQ stands for lesbian, gay, bisexual, transgender, and queer or questioning.

perform: To entertain people by singing, acting, or doing some other activity that requires skill.

personality: The set of qualities and ways of behaving that make a person different from other people.

platform: An application or website that serves as a base from which a service is provided.

publish: To print a written work and present it to the public.

represent: To serve as an example of.

role: A part, job, or function.

traditional: Following what's been done for a long time.

FOR MORE INFORMATION

WEBSITES

JoJo Siwa Official Site

itsjojosiwa.com

This is JoJo Siwa's official website, which features facts about her life and work and links to her social media pages.

YouTube: XOMG POP!

www.youtube.com/@itsxomgpop

JoJo's official YouTube channel is now the place to find her videos as well as videos of XOMG POP!—the group she helped create.

BOOKS

Rusick, Jessica. *JoJo Siwa*. Minneapolis, MN: Checkerboard Library, 2020.

Schwartz, Heather E. *JoJo Siwa: Fan Favorite*. Minneapolis, MN: Lerner Publications, 2021.

Siwa, JoJo. *JoJo's Guide to the Sweet Life: #PeaceOutHaterz*. New York, NY: Amulet Books, 2020.

INDEX